The Glorious History of the United States

From Columbus to the Afghan war

Jagath Jayaprakash

**The Glorious History of the United States:
From Columbus to the Afghan war**

Jagath Jayaprakash

History

Edited, Printed & Published by:
Jagath Jayaprakash

First Published:
March 2023

Honest Books
Geethalayam
Pattamthuruthu,
Kollam-691601
Kerala, India
Phone: +91 8075374584

Email id: jagathjp86@gmail.com

Contents

Introduction

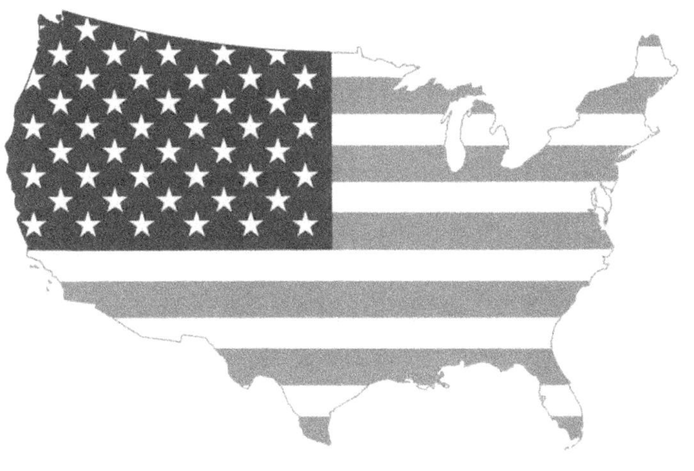

1/US Flag Map

The United States, officially known as the United States of America, abbreviated U.S. or U.S.A., occasionally known as America, is a country in North America, a federal republic comprised of 50 states. Aside from the 48 contiguous states that occupy the continent's main latitudes, the United States also contains the state of Alaska, located at the far northwestern tip of North America, and the island state of Hawaii, which is located in the mid-Pacific Ocean. Canada borders the conterminous states on the North, the Atlantic Ocean on the East, the Gulf of Mexico and Mexico on the South, and the Pacific Ocean on the West. The United States is the world's fourth-largest land area (after Russia, Canada, and China).

The United States has been a country of immigrants throughout its history. The population is varied, with individuals arriving worldwide searching for safety and a better way of life. New England, the mid-Atlantic, the South, the Midwest, the Southwest, and the West are the six regions of the United States. European immigrants arrived in New England seeking religious liberty. Connecticut, Maine, Massachusetts, New Hampshire, Rhode Island, and Vermont are among them. Delaware, Maryland, New Jersey, New York, Pennsylvania, and Washington, D.C. are all mid-Atlantic areas. These industrial sectors drew millions of European immigrants and gave rise to some of the largest cities on the East Coast. These industrial sectors drew millions of European immigrants and gave rise to some of the major cities on the East Coast, comprising New York, Baltimore, and Philadelphia.

The Midwest is known as the "breadbasket" of the

United States since it is home to the majority of the country's agricultural base. Illinois, Indiana, Iowa, Kansas, Michigan, Minnesota, Missouri, Nebraska, North Dakota, Ohio, South Dakota, and Wisconsin make up the area.

The Southwest has a stunning panorama of prairie and desert. The Southwest states of Arizona, New Mexico, Oklahoma, and Texas are home to some of the world's great natural wonders, such as the Grand Canyon and Carlsbad Caverns.

Alabama, Arkansas, Florida, Georgia, Kentucky, Louisiana, Mississippi, North Carolina, South Carolina, Tennessee, Virginia, and West Virginia are all South. All battled following the Civil War, which lasted from 1860 to 1865.

For more than 200 years, the history of the United States has been an experiment in democracy. Issues addressed in the early years are still being discussed and resolved today: big government against small government, individual rights versus collective rights, uncontrolled capitalism versus regulated trade and labour, and global participation versus isolationism. With its rolling plains and cowboys, the American West symbolizes the country's pioneering spirit. The West is varied, encompassing everything from vast wilderness to the desolate desert, coral reefs to Arctic tundra, and Hollywood to Yellowstone. Alaska, Colorado, California, Hawaii, Idaho,

Montana, Nevada, Oregon, Utah, Washington, and Wyoming are Western states.

2 /Map of the United States

The Post-Colonial America

The last Ice Age occurred roughly 35,000 years ago. Much of the world's water had been frozen into massive ice sheets. A 1,500-kilometre-long land bridge connected Asia and North America. Humans colonized much of what is now the Americas 12,000 years ago.

The first "Americans" arrived from Asia through a land bridge. Historians think they lived for thousands of years in what is now Alaska. They went south into what is now the United States of America.

They resided near the Pacific Ocean in the Northwest, in the Southwest's mountains and deserts, and in the Midwest's Mississippi River valley.

Hohokam, Adenans, Hopewellians, and Anasazi are the names given to these early groups. They established settlements and cultivated crops. Their lives were intertwined with the Earth. They placed a great value on family and community. According to history, they recounted stories and transmitted knowledge mostly through conversation rather than writing. Hieroglyphics was a type of expressive writing utilized by some. Nature played a vital role in their spiritual beliefs. Some cultures erected massive dirt heaps in the shape of snakes, birds, or pyramids.

The various factions traded with one another, but they also battled.

Nobody knows why these tribes vanished.

Other groups, including the Hopi and Zuni, eventually settled in this area and flourished. Around two million native people lived in what is now the United States when the first Europeans arrived.

Historians reason the Norse were the first Europeans to arrive. They had travelled from Greenland, where Erik the Red had established a colony in 985. Erik's son, Leif, visited the northeast coast of what is now Canada in 1001.

Remains of Norse homes were discovered in northern Newfoundland.

Other Europeans took about 500 years to reach North America and another 100 years to establish permanent colonies. The initial explorers had little knowledge of America. They were seeking a means to go by sea from Europe to Asia. Later arrivals from Europe—mostly Spanish and Portuguese, but also Dutch, French, and British—came in search of land and the riches of the "New World."

Christopher Columbus was the most famous explorer. Although he was Italian, Queen Isabella of Spain paid for his travels. In 1492, Columbus arrived on the Caribbean Sea islands. He never made it to what is now known as the United States.

In 1497, an adventurer travelling for England named John Cabot arrived in eastern Canada. With his landing, the British secured a claim to territory in North America.

Spain explored and claimed more land in the Americas than any other country throughout the 1500s. Juan Ponce de Léon arrived in Florida in 1513. In 1539, Hernando De Soto arrived in Florida and explored the Mississippi River.

In 1522, Spain invaded Mexico. Francisco Vázquez de Coronado set out in 1540 to locate the legendary Seven Cities of Cibola. He began his search in Mexico, then moved north to the Grand Canyon in Arizona and onto the Great Plains.

Others, like Giovanni da Verrazano, Jacques Cartier, and Amerigo Vespucci, ventured further north. Amerigo Vespucci was the name given to the two American continents.

The Spanish established the first permanent European settlement in North America. It was constructed in St. Augustine, Florida. Thirteen British colonies to the North would eventually combine to establish the United States. Virginia and Massachusetts were the first to do so.

Not only did explorers establish themselves in the New World. People began to go to the New World to live. These folks were European immigrants.

3/The Pilgrims landing on Plymouth Rock, December 1620

Virginia Algonquian man, 1645

4/Algonquian Native American

The Colonial Era

In the 1600s, the majority of individuals who came to the British colonies were English.

Others emanated from the Netherlands, Sweden, Germany, France, Scotland, and Northern Ireland, among other places. By 1690, there were 250,000 individuals in the New World. There were 2.5 million individuals in 1790.

People assembled for a variety of reasons. Some people fled their houses to avoid the fighting. Others want political or religious liberty. Some had to labour as servants to recoup the expense of their journey before being released. Some arrived as slaves, such as black Africans.

Over time, the 13 colonies grew into three different areas. The colonists were astonishingly productive. Early marriages and big families were promoted by economic opportunity, particularly in easily accessible land. Bachelors and unmarried women could not live comfortably and were in short supply. Widows and widowers needed partners to keep their houses and raise their children, so many remarried rapidly. As a result, most individuals were married, children were plentiful, and households of ten or more members were frequent. Despite suffering enormous losses due to sickness and hardship, the colonists multiplied. Their numbers were further boosted by continued immigration from the United Kingdom and Europe west of the Elbe River.

The early settlements were located along the Atlantic coast and on rivers that poured into the sea. Water power was accessible in the Northeast, where trees covered the slopes and stones filled the soil. New England was the name given to the region of the Northeast that encompassed Massachusetts, Connecticut, and Rhode Island.

The colonies were regarded as a country of hope in Britain and continental Europe. Furthermore, both the country and the colonies promoted immigration by incentivizing individuals who would cross the seas. Foreign Protestants were especially welcomed in the colonies. Furthermore, many individuals were forced to come to America, including criminals, political prisoners, and enslaved Africans. Every generation, the American population doubled.

The settlement of the Atlantic coast was influenced by several factors, including political, religious, and economic considerations. By 1600, both labour and capital in England had become very mobile and were looking for new profitable domains. Many people were dissatisfied with the sharp rise in prices and living costs; the surge in sheep grazing and the fencing of past common lands flock many from the soil; and bold young men, comprising younger sons of the upper class, who had lost in peace the occupation that the wars with Spain had given them, looked abroad.

Timber, fishing, shipbuilding, and commerce were the mainstays of the economy.

New York, New Jersey, Pennsylvania, Maryland and Delaware were among the middle colonies.

The weather was nicer, and the scenery was more diversified. People worked in manufacturing and agriculture. Society had become more diversified and sophisticated. People moved to New York from throughout Europe.

Virginia, Georgia, North Carolina, and South Carolina were among the southern colonies. The growing season was long, and the soil was rich in nutrients. The majority of individuals were farmers. Some had tiny farms that they worked on their own. The affluent farmers owned enormous plantations and used African slaves.

There were both good and terrible ties between settlers and Native Americans (also known as Indians).

The two tribes traded and were cordial in various regions. In most cases, as the settlements got larger, the Indians were compelled to relocate.

Over time, all of the colonies established administrations modelled on the British tradition of public engagement. The Glorious Revolution of 1688–1689 in Britain reduced the king's power while giving more power to the people. The American colonists keenly noted these developments. Colonial assemblies claimed the authority to operate as local legislatures. They enacted legislation that reduced the power of the royal governor while increasing their authority.

Disagreements remained between the royal governors and the legislatures. The colonists learned that their interests frequently differed from those of Britain. Initially, the colonists desired self-government within the framework of a British commonwealth.

They didn't seek independence until much later.

5/The Leiden history piece

The Path to Independence

The concepts of liberalism and democracy serve as the foundation of the American political system. As the colonists constructed their new community, their faith in these beliefs became stronger. During the 1700s, Britain's 13 colonies gained population and economic power. Despite being administered by a remote administration, the colonists were in charge of many local issues.

Between 1660 and 1740, three important new forces emerged to change the British possessions in North America. They were the economic rules reflected in the Acts of Trade and Navigation, the partial systematization of imperial administration, and the fight with the French for supremacy over the continent. By the year 1700, the colonists had probably reached over 250,000 and were multiplying at a rate that has seldom been matched in the history of Western countries. Immigration, early marriages, the economic worth of children in an agricultural community, and a relatively high level of health accelerated this rise.

After Britain won an expensive war with France in the 1750s, the colonists were required to contribute to the war's and Britain's vast empire's costs. These policies hampered the colonists' way of life.

The Royal Proclamation of 1763, for example, prohibited colonists from settling on new land. The Currency Act of 1764 made it unlawful in the colonies to create paper money.

The Quartering Act of 1765 mandates colonists to provide food and shelter for royal soldiers. The Stamp Act of 1765 levied all legal documents, licenses, periodicals, and leases.

The Stamp Act galvanized the colonists into a concerted opposition movement. The fundamental issue was that they were barred from participating in the government that taxed them.

Twenty-seven representatives from nine colonies gathered in New York in October 1765. They issued resolutions stating that separate colonies should be allowed to levy their taxes. Most of the delegates were happy, but a tiny group of radicals desired independence from Britain.

Samuel Adams of Massachusetts was one of them. He delivered talks and authored newspaper articles. The groups he assisted in organizing formed an important aspect of the revolutionary struggle.

By 1773, colonial business people dissatisfied with

British supervision of the tea trade were intrigued by Sam Adams' theories. In December 1773, a group of men snuck into three British ships in Boston port and tossed the tea shipment overboard. The Boston Tea Party arose as a result of this occurrence.

The British Parliament penalized Massachusetts by blocking the port of Boston and limiting local autonomy. The new laws were dubbed the Intolerable Acts by colonists, who banded together to fight them. Except for Georgia, all the colonies sent delegations to Philadelphia in September 1774 to discuss their "current sad position." The First Continental Congress was held in 1776.

Early in 1763, King George III and his ministers declared the Seven Years' War triumphantly over and launched the first lengthy steps toward another struggle that would shock the British Empire to its core. Fifteen days after the Treaty of Paris was signed, the secretary of war announced in the House of Commons a ministerial plan to increase the British garrison forces in North America from 3,100 men to 7,500, declaring that these troops would "be supported the first year by England, then by the Colonies." This straightforward proposition produced concerns that progressively pushed the American colonies toward independence.

Colonists were enraged that the British had stripped them of their rights, but not everyone agreed on a remedy. Loyalists desired to remain subjects of the monarch. Moderates desired to reach a compromise and improve ties with the British administration. The revolutionaries want total independence.

They began gathering weapons and preparing men in preparation for the war for freedom.

6/British General Burgoyne's surrender at Saratoga in the American Revolution

7 /George Washington

Revolution for Freedom

When confronted with Parliament's actions, which became known as the Townshend Acts, the Americans resisted once more, but with less unanimity than during the Stamp Act troubles, because many cautious colonists, particularly men of property who had been worried by the rioting of 1765–66, were not inclined to struggle vigorously. The Americans had not previously stated that their objection to taxation without representation applied to both tariffs collected at their ports and the stamp tax.

However, an unsettling occurrence occurred in Boston on the same day North introduced his repeal bill. Because the royal governor, Thomas Hutchinson, requested that troops be retained in Boston, some of those dispatched there remained until March 1770. Tensions between soldiers and citizens grew, culminating in the Boston Massacre on March 5. British soldiers were attacked by civilians throwing stones and ice at them, killing three Bostonians and mortally wounding two others. A Boston jury convicted two of the soldiers of manslaughter, and the men's bloodshed exacerbated the chasm between Britain and America.

The American Revolution and the battle for independence from Britain started with a brief clash between British forces and Americans on April 19, 1775. The British forces departed Boston, Massachusetts, intending to steal guns and ammunition from the revolutionary colonists. The Minutemen were told to evacuate by the British. The colonists complied, but as they were leaving, someone fired a shot. The British forces used weapons and bayonets to fight the Minutemen.

As the British soldiers returned to Boston in their brilliant red uniforms, fighting broke out in various spots along the road. Over 250 "redcoats" were killed or injured. The Americans suffered a total of 93 casualties.

The Second Continental Congress convened in Philadelphia, and colonial representatives rushed there. More than half of the people opted to go to war with Britain. They resolved to combine the colonial troops into a single army. George Washington of Virginia was appointed as commander-in-chief.

At the same time, they submitted a peace resolution to King George III to prevent a conflict. The king rejected it. The monarch declared the American colonies to be in rebellion on August 23, 1775.

The urge for freedom became stronger during the following few months. In his treatise, Common Sense, Thomas Paine, a radical political theorist, campaigned for independence and against the hereditary monarchy. He proposed two conceivable scenarios for the United States. People may continue to be unequal citizens under a monarch or live in an independent country with dreams of liberty and happiness.

The Second Continental Congress formed a committee to draft a declaration outlining the colonies' grievances against the monarch and their resolve to secede from Britain. The justifications were based on concepts from France and the United Kingdom.

Thomas Jefferson mostly wrote the Declaration of Independence.

The Declaration of Independence announced the world as a new nation and its views on human liberty. It contended that political rights are fundamental human rights that apply to everyone. The Second Continental Congress, on July 4, 1776, adopted this document. In the United States, the Fourth of July became known as Independence Day.

The colonies and the United Kingdom went to war. General Washington's forces were beaten in New York, and British soldiers gained possession of Philadelphia, forcing the Second Continental Congress to escape. The Continental Army triumphed in Saratoga, New York, and Princeton and Trenton, New Jersey. George Washington had difficulty obtaining the personnel and supplies he required to win the war.

France recognized the United States as a sovereign entity and signed an alliance pact with them in 1778. France aided the U.S. in undermining Britain, its long-time adversary. Battles raged from Montreal, Canada, to Savannah, Georgia. In 1781, a massive British army surrendered at Yorktown, Virginia. On April 15, 1783, a peace deal was signed in Paris, bringing the conflict to a conclusion. Britain and other nations acknowledged the United States as an independent entity in this treaty. The Revolution had an impact on more than just North America.

The concept of natural rights grew in popularity throughout the Western world. Famous leaders like Thaddeus Kosciusko (Poland), Friedrich von Steuben (Prussia), and the Marquis de Lafayette (France) spread the concept of liberty throughout their respective countries.

The Treaty of Paris established the 13 colonies as nations, but uniting the colonies remained.

*8/ The Peace Hat and The Tomb of the Unknown
Revolutionary War Soldier*

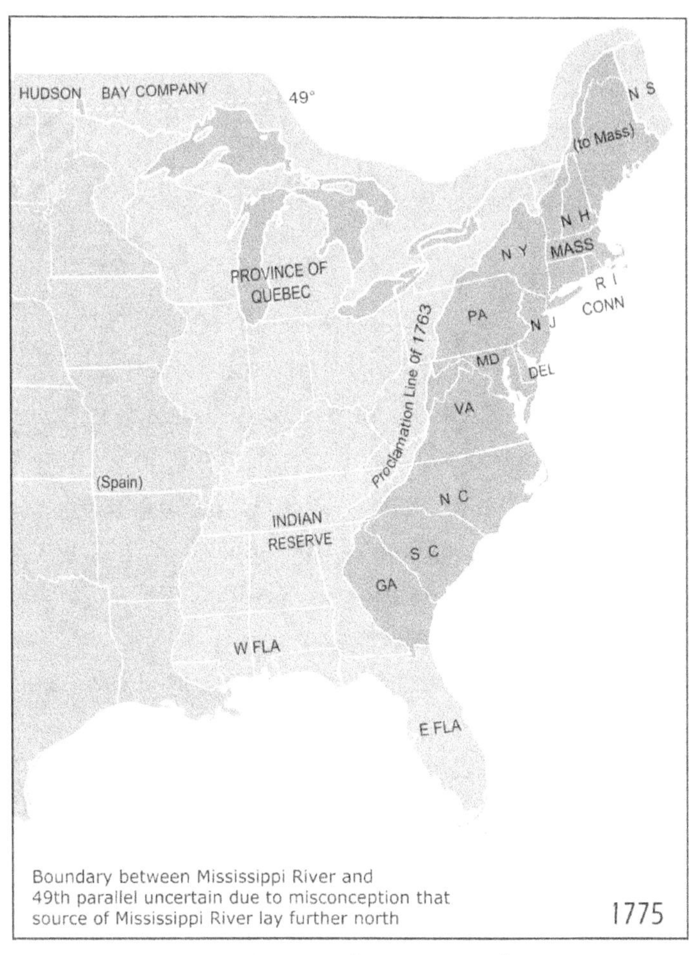

9/ The Thirteen Colonies (shown in red) in 1775, /New England (New Hampshire; Massachusetts; Rhode Island; Connecticut); Middle (New York; New Jersey; Pennsylvania; Delaware); Southern (Maryland; Virginia; North Carolina; South Carolina; and Georgia)

Establishing a National Government

The Revolution had an impact on more than just North America. The concept of natural rights grew in popularity throughout the Western world. Famous leaders like Thaddeus Kosciusko (Poland), Friedrich von Steuben (Prussia), and the Marquis de Lafayette (France) spread the concept of liberty throughout their respective countries.

The Treaty of Paris established the 13 colonies as nations, but uniting the colonies remained.

Every state had its currency, army, and navy. Each country traded and collaborated with other countries. Each state collected taxes in its unique manner. Each state thought that its path was the correct one.

It was a 13-country nation. The 13 states, according to Alexander Hamilton of New York, needed to reconsider the Confederation. He and others proposed holding a major assembly to accomplish this.

Fifty-five delegates convened in Philadelphia in May 1787. They were well-versed in history, law, and political philosophy and were familiar with colonial and state governments.

Most people thought the Articles of Confederation were ineffective. They offered a constitution that outlined a new system of government based on independent legislative, executive, and judicial powers. The delegates did not reach an agreement on all of the specifics.

Many delegates desired a strong central government that would limit the sovereignty of states. Others thought that a weak national government was preferable. They desired increased authority for the states.

Some delegates wanted fewer individuals to vote because they considered most people had the education needed to make sound judgments. Delegates from minor states aspired for equal representation in the next Congress.

Delegates from large states urged that their states be given more clout. Some delegates from states where slavery was outlawed or not extensively practised desired that slavery be made illegal throughout the country. Delegates from states where slave labour was prevalent declined to attend.

Some delegates desired that the newly colonized regions to the West be recognized as states. Others were not convinced. The delegates deliberated for four months before reaching an agreement. The Constitution established the foundation for the new government. The national government could print money, levy taxes, negotiate with foreign governments, maintain an army, establish a postal system, and fight the war. To prevent the government from growing too powerful, the United States Constitution separated it into three equal parts: a legislature (Congress), an executive (President), and a judicial system (Supreme Court). Each portion sought to ensure that the other sections did not usurp the authority that belonged to them.

The majority of the representatives signed the new Constitution on September 17, 1787. They decided that when nine of the thirteen states ratified or approved the Constitution, it would become the law of the United States.

The Constitution took roughly a year to be ratified. The country was split into two halves. The Federalists desired a strong central government. They backed the Constitution. The anti-Federalists desired a loose confederation of states. They were concerned that a powerful central government would become totalitarian. They were opposed to the Constitution.

After it was approved, some Americans stated that individual rights were not enumerated in the Constitution.

When the United States was founded, In September 1789, Congress gathered in New York City, and the representatives presented a lot of constitutional modifications to

These rights should be listed. They made ten changes. The Bill of Rights is also known as the Declaration of Rights. The First Amendment guarantees freedom of expression.

The freedom of expression, the press, religion, and the right to demonstrate, gather peacefully, and demand change.

The Fourth Amendment protects citizens against unjustified searches and seizures. In criminal proceedings, the Fifth Amendment guarantees due process of law. In the more than 200 years since the Bill of Rights, only 17 amendments have been added to the Constitution.

10 /Philadelphia – Old City: Independence Hall – The
Signing of the Constitution

11/Francis Scott Key reaches out towards the flag in
"The Star–Spangled Banner" by Percy Moran

Early Years and Westward Extension

On April 30, 1789, George Washington was inaugurated as the first President of the United States. He was in command of the army. His task as President was to establish a functioning administration. He established the Treasury, Justice, and War departments in collaboration with Congress. The cabinet refers to the leaders of these departments as well as those that were established afterwards.

The Supreme Court consisted of one chief justice and five (now eight) associate justices. Three circuit courts and thirteen district courts were established—policies for administering the western regions and admitting them to the Union as new states were devised.

Before leaving office, George Washington served two four-year terms as President. (Only one President of the United States, Franklin D. Roosevelt, has served more than two terms.) Today, the Constitution prohibits anybody from being elected President more than twice.) The following two presidents,

John Adams and Thomas Jefferson, held opposing views on the function of government.

As a result, political parties were formed.

John Adams and Alexander Hamilton led the Federalists. People involved in commerce and industry were among their supporters. They believed in the power of a strong central government. The majority of their support came from the North. Jefferson was the Republican Party's leader. Many farmers were among their backers. They were opposed to a strong central government. They felt that states should have more power. They had a lot of support in the South.

For approximately 20 years, the United States remained friendly to other countries and neutral in their problems, while France and Britain were at war once more.

The British navy intercepted American ships en route to France. The French navy intercepted American ships en route to Britain.

After years of futile diplomacy, the United States declared war on Britain in 1812. The engagements were largely fought in the Northeastern states and along the East Coast. A portion of the British troops arrived in Washington, DC, the future capital of the United States.

Soldiers set fire to the White House. As the White House burnt, President James Madison escaped.

The westward movement of Europeans inside the continental bounds of the mainland United States began immediately after the first colonial colonies were founded along the Atlantic coast. The early British immigrants in the New World remained near the Atlantic, which served as their lifeline to essential supplies from England. However, by the 1630s, Massachusetts Bay colonists were forcing their way into the Connecticut River valley. Despite resistance from the French and Native Americans, northern American colonists had controlled much of New England by the 1750s.

The Americans won significant fights both on land and at sea. Exhausted and in debt after its previous war with France, Britain negotiated a peace deal with the United States in 1815. The triumph of the United States ensured that Britain would not develop colonies south of the Canadian border.

Many of the fledgling nation's difficulties had subsided by 1815. The United States had a balance between liberty and order under the Constitution. The country's national debt was modest. Much of the continent remained unexplored. The country was at peace, prosperous, and making social progress.

The Monroe Doctrine was a significant addition to international policy. President James Monroe's declaration of sympathy with newly independent Central and South American states served as a warning to Europe not to pursue colonies in Latin America.

Despite decades of pushing the frontier line westward, it wasn't until the end of the War of 1812 that the westward movement became a massive outpouring of people throughout the continent. By 1830, the Old Northwest and Old Southwest, which had been sparsely inhabited before the war, had attracted enough inhabitants to justify the admission of Illinois, Indiana, Missouri, Alabama, and Mississippi as states to the Union.

The United States expanded in size when it purchased the Louisiana Territory from France in 1803 and Florida from Spain in 1819. Six new states were formed between 1816 and 1821. The population quadrupled between 1812 and 1852.

As the country grew, the disparities between the states became increasingly apparent. The United States was a country with civilized cities but lawless borders. The United States cherished liberty while tolerating slavery. The discrepancies began to cause issues.

12/A miner strikes gold in California

13/ National Atlas of the United States/ The Territorial acquisitions of the United States, such as the Thirteen Colonies, the Louisiana Purchase, British and Spanish Cession, and so on

The Clash within the United States

The United States was a big country rich with contrasts in 1850. Finance, trade, shipping, and manufacturing were centred in New England and the Middle Atlantic states. Lumber, equipment, and textiles were among their offerings. Many plantations in the southern states employed slave labour to cultivate tobacco, sugar, and cotton. Farms existed in the Middle Western nations as well, although free men worked them.

Missouri applied to become a state in 1819. Northerners were opposed because the area housed 10,000 slaves. Because the Constitution granted each new state the right to elect two senators, new states had the potential to shift the political balance between "free" and "slave" states. Congressman Henry Clay proposed a solution that would satisfy both the North and the South. Missouri would become a slave state.

The years leading up to the Civil War (1820–1860, or the "antebellum years") were among the most turbulent in American history, with tremendous changes taking place as the country matured. During these years, the country was converted from a rural and frontiersman nation to an urbanized economic powerhouse. Five primary themes dominated American economic, social, and political life during this Century as the industrialized North and agrarian South drifted apart.

Between 1820 and 1840, the Market Revolution happened—the transition from an agrarian economy to one based on salaries and the trade of commodities and services—completely transformed the northern and western economies.

During this period, American culture urbanized dramatically. The United States had previously been a region dominated by farmers, but around 1820, millions of people began to migrate to cities. Along with millions of Irish and German immigrants, they flocked to northern cities, searching for work in the new industrial economy. Because it gave rise to America's first middle class, the introduction of the wage labour system had a significant role in changing the social fabric. This increasing middle class, comprised primarily of white-collar employees and skilled labourers, became the driving force behind many reform campaigns.

During the antebellum period, the principal political fights centred on state rights. Southern states were controlled by "states' righters," or those who felt that individual states should have the last say in questions of constitutional interpretation. In his "South Carolina Exposition and Protest" article, John C. Calhoun claimed, inspired by the old Democratic-Republicans, that states had the authority to nullify legislation they deemed illegal since the states had drafted the Constitution. Others, including President Andrew Jackson and Chief Justice John Marshall, thought the federal government had power over the states.

The struggle over slavery—the most controversial issue the nation had yet faced—was inextricably linked to the states' rights question. Between 1820 and 1860, northerners became increasingly aware of the horrors and inequities of slavery, while southerners became increasingly reliant on it to maintain their cotton-based economy. Northerners did not necessarily seek social and political equality for blacks; rather, they desired freedom. The political discussion focused on the westward extension of slavery, which southern elites considered critical to continuing their aristocratic social and economic order. Others were passionately opposed to the spread of slavery outside of the South.

Maine would become a slave-free state. The Missouri Compromise was agreed upon.

In the years that followed, each side became increasingly certain in their ideas. Many Northerners believed that slavery was sinful. Others viewed it as a danger to free labour. Slavery was regarded as a way of life by the majority of white Southerners.

Thousands of slaves fled to the North with the assistance of individuals who travelled along hidden routes known as the Underground railroad. However, one-third of the entire population of slave states was not free in 1860.

During the antebellum years, the question of westward expansion had a major impact on American politics and culture. Following the War of 1812, many patriots thought that God meant to bring democracy and Protestantism to the whole continent. Over a million Americans were inspired by the concept of "manifest destiny" to sell their houses in the East and embark on perilous Oregon, Mormon, Santa Fe, and California Trails. Policymakers used public opinion to capture Florida and Oregon, and in 1846, they made war on Mexico to seize Texas, California, and all in between.

Most Northerners were unconcerned with slavery in the South, but they opposed slavery in the new territories. The Southerners argued that these regions had the right to determine whether or not to legalize slavery. A young politician from Illinois thought that this was a national, not a local, problem. Abraham Lincoln was his name. Although he agreed that the South might keep its slaves, he campaigned to keep slavery out of the territories. Lincoln believed that slavery would be abolished over time. "A divided house cannot stand," he remarked. "This government cannot continue to be half-slave and half-free indefinitely."

If Lincoln was elected President, the South threatened to abandon the Union. Before Lincoln became President, some Southern states began to leave the Union after he won the election.

14/Lincoln's Emancipation Proclamation was issued on January 1, 1863

Civil War and Post-Battle Rebuilding

The American Civil War commenced in April 1861. The South asserted its right to secede from the United States, sometimes known as the Union, and create its Confederacy. President Lincoln commanded the Northern states. He was adamant about putting an end to the revolt and keeping the country unified.

In America's historical awareness, the Civil War is a pivotal event. While the Revolution of 1776-1783 established the United States, the Civil War of 1861-1865 decided the country's nature. The war resolved two vital questions left unresolved by the Revolution: whether the United States was to be a dissolvable confederation of sovereign states or an amalgamated nation with a sovereign national government, and whether this nation, born of a declaration that all men were created equal, would continue to be existent as the world's largest slaveholding country.

The North possessed a larger population, more raw materials for manufacturing war supplies, and a stronger railway infrastructure. The South had

more experienced military officers and a better un-
derstanding of the battlefields as most of the war was
battled in the South.

The conflict lasted four years. Tens of thousands
of soldiers battled on land and at sea.

The deadliest day of the conflict was September 17, 1862. The two armies clashed in Maryland
at Antietam Creek. General Robert E. Lee and his
Confederate Army were unable to push back Union
soldiers headed by Gen. George McClellan. Lee and
his troops escaped.

Although the fight was not decisive, it was politi-
cally significant. Britain and France had prepared to
recognize the Confederacy, but they postponed their
decision. The South was never given the assistance
it sorely required.

Later the same year, in 1862, President Lincoln
issued a preliminary Emancipation Proclamation,
freeing all slaves in the Confederate states. It also
permitted the recruitment of African Americans into
the Union Army. The North sought to preserve the
Union and abolish slavery.

The North began to win significant battles. As his
army marched into Georgia and South Carolina in
1864, Gen. William T. Sherman created a trail of
destruction (known as the scorched-earth doctrine).
Gen. Lee submitted to Union Gen. Ulysses S. Grant in
Virginia in April 1865. The Civil War has ended. The

Civil War claimed the lives of more Americans than any other U.S. battle.

A Confederate sympathizer assassinated President Lincoln less than a week after the South surrendered.

Vice President Andrew Johnson was sworn in as President with the task of reconciling the country. Johnson was from the South. He granted pardons to several Southerners, restoring their political privileges.

By 1865, most former Confederate states had nullified their secession actions but refused to abolish slavery. Except for Tennessee, all Confederate states refused to grant African American men full citizenship.

In retaliation, Republicans in Congress refused to allow rebel leaders to take office. The Union generals who ruled the South barred anybody who refused to swear an oath of allegiance to the Union from voting. Congress vigorously backed African American rights.

Many of these programs were opposed by President Johnson. The House impeached Johnson, but the Senate fell one vote short of the two-thirds majority needed to remove Johnson from office. He was re-elected President, although he began to cave more frequently to the Republican Congress.

The Southern states were barred from sending members to Congress until they approved constitutional amendments prohibiting slavery, providing all residents "equal protection of the laws," and granting all male citizens the right to vote regardless of race.

Northern victory in the conflict maintained the United States as a unified nation and put an end to slavery, which had split the country from its inception. However, these deeds came at the cost of 625,000 lives—nearly as many as American soldiers perished in all previous conflicts combined. Between the finale of the Napoleonic Wars in 1815 and the outbreak of World War I in 1914, the American Civil War was the largest and most devastating conflict in the Western world.

Reconstruction, in American history, is the period following the American Civil War during which efforts were made to redress the discriminations of slavery and its political, social, and economic legacies, as well as to solve the problems ascending from the readmission to the Union of the 11 states that had seceded at or before the outburst of the war. Many historians had long characterized Reconstruction as when angry Radical Republicans imposed Black dominance on the vanquished Confederacy. Still, since the late twentieth century, it has been seen more warmly as a praiseworthy experiment in interracial democracy. Reconstruction brought about significant changes in America's political life.

For a while, these changes resulted in significant

gains for African Americans in the South. When the North pulled out its army from the Southern states, particularly in the late 1870s, white Southerners recovered political control and denied new Southern blacks new rights. Although blacks in the South were free, local laws denied them their rights. They had the right to vote, but they were scared to utilize it because of the danger of violence. Southern governments implemented "segregation," which compelled blacks and whites to utilize separate public facilities, such as schools and water fountains. Not unexpectedly, the "black" restrooms were inferior to the "white" restrooms.

15/ Confederate dead before the Dunker Church

16/A depiction of San Juan Hill's storming from the Spanish–American War

Growth and Transformation

The United States transformed soon after the Civil War, and the border was becoming less wild. Cities expanded in size and population.

There were more industries, steel mills, and railways developed. Immigrants approached the United States with hopes of a better life.

At the end of the war, the South was a shattered territory, burdened by debt and demoralized by racial violence. Over time, it became clear that drastic rebuilding, stringent regulations, and ongoing hostility against former Confederates were not resolving the South's issues. Congress approved a comprehensive Amnesty Act in May 1872, restoring full political rights to everyone except around 500 Confederate supporters.

The United States of America was changed from a rural republic to an urban state between the Civil War and World War I. The country rose to prominence as an industrial powerhouse. The region was defined by massive industries and steel mills, thriving cities, and enormous agricultural holdings. The first transcontinental railroad was built in 1869, and by 1900, the United States had more rail miles than the whole of Europe combined. Petroleum, steel, and textile sectors thrived. This was the Golden Age of Invention. Alexander Graham Bell invented the telephone, Edison created the light bulb, and George Eastman created the moving picture, which was eventually referred to as a film. Before 1860, the government granted 36,000 patents. Between 1860 and 1890, the government printed 440,000 stamps.

On the other hand, the South remained generally impoverished, primarily agricultural, and economically reliant even thirty years after the Civil War. Its civilization imposed strict social segregation of blacks and whites and condoned racial violence regularly.

By 1890, the border had vanished. The government's objective had been to relocate Indians beyond the reach of the white border, but reservations had grown smaller and more congested, and tribal treaty rights were frequently misused. The United States expanded its influence and its domain across widely dispersed territories in the Atlantic and Pacific Oceans and into Central America during the latter decades of the nineteenth century. Alaska was bought from Russia by the United States in 1867.

Independent firms combined to form larger corporations, which are frequently referred to as trusts. This was particularly true in the steel, rail, oil, and communications industries. Buyers had fewer options, and corporations had greater influence as there were fewer enterprises. To prevent monopolies, antitrust legislation was enacted in 1890, although it proved ineffective.

Farming remained the most common employment in America, and Scientists enhanced seeds. New machines did some of the jobs that men had done. Farmers in the United States produced enough grain, pork, cotton, and wool to transport the excess elsewhere.

There was still an opportunity for exploration and new colonies in the Western areas. Miners discovered ore and gold in the mountains, and Sheep farmers established themselves in river valleys. The Great Plains became a haven for food growers, and Ranchers allowed their livestock to roam on the expansive pastures. Cowboys herded large herds of cattle to the train to be sent to the East. The "Wild West" depicted in numerous cowboy stories and movies was barely around for 30 years.

When Europeans first landed on the East Coast, they drove the indigenous people west. Each time, the government offered fresh territory to the indigenous people to have a place to live. The pledges were breached each time as white settlers stole the land.

Sioux tribes in the Northern Plains and Apaches in the Southwest clashed in the late 1800s. Despite their might, U.S. government troops defeated them. Many tribes would be housed on reservations, which are government grounds managed by Indian tribes. There are now over 300 bookings.

Toward the close of the nineteenth century, European countries invaded Africa and struggled to trade in Asia. Many Americans thought that the U.S. should follow suit. Many other Americans were opposed to any move that appeared imperialistic.

Following a brief war with Spain in 1898, the United States gained control of many Spanish territories, including Cuba, Puerto Rico, Guam, and the Philippines. Officially, the U.S. urged them to become self-sufficient. In actuality, the U.S. maintained control.

Foreign policy ideology coexisted, intending to prevent European nations from obtaining territory that would allow them to project military strength against the United States. Americans were likewise looking for new markets in which to sell their wares. By the close of the nineteenth century, the United States established itself as a rising world force.

17/George M. Cohan's song "Over There" captured the patriotic mood of the time

Disgruntlement and Transformation

The United States had seen expansion, civil conflict, economic success, and economic hardship by 1900. Americans believed in religious liberty, and the majority of people had access to free public education. The free press persisted.

The installation of President William McKinley in 1897 appeared to herald the end of an age of political strife and the start of a new era of unsurpassed tranquillity. After the disastrous panic of 1893, prosperity was returning. The agrarian insurrection led by Bryan in the election of 1896 had been defeated, and the national government was safely in the hands of large business supporters. The Dingley Tariff Act of 1897 significantly increased tariff rates; the Gold Standard Act of 1897 crushed the dreams of proponents of free coinage of silver; McKinley did little to prevent a series of business mergers in violation of the Sherman Antitrust Act.

On the negative side, it frequently appeared that political authority belonged to a few corrupt politicians and their business associates. As a result, the concept of Progressivism was formed. Progressives desired more democracy and fairness. They want an honest government that would limit the dominance of business.

This generation of Americans likewise wished for a more democratic world. At home, this meant granting women the right to vote and instituting a slew of electoral changes, including recall, referendum, and direct election of Senators. Abroad, it meant attempting to make the globe more democratic. In 1917, the United States went into the war against authoritarian Germany and Austria-Hungary led by the United Kingdom and France, both democratic states. Soon after World War I, most Americans abandoned caring for international affairs, adopting a "live and let live" mentality. President Theodore Roosevelt (1901–1909) was a supporter of Progressivism. He collaborated with Congress to control monopolistic corporations. He also fought tirelessly to safeguard the country's natural resources.

Changes were carried on by the future presidents, particularly Woodrow Wilson (1913–1921). The Federal Reserve banking system regulated interest rates and the money supply. The Federal Trade Commission dealt with unfair commercial practices. New legislation improved working conditions for sailors and railroad workers. Farmers now have greater knowledge and access to loans. Import taxes have been reduced or removed.

Further immigrants arrived in the United States during the Progressive Era. Between 1890 and 1921, about 19 million immigrants immigrated from Russia, Poland, Greece, Canada, Italy, Mexico, and Japan.

By the 1920s, residents were concerned that immigrants would take their jobs and alter the culture of the United States. Although the government established quotas to limit immigration, it lifted those limitations in the 1960s, ensuring that the United States would remain where individuals of many backgrounds and cultures could construct an American identity.

The 1920s, often known as the "roaring twenties" and "the new period," were comparable to the Progressive Era in that America's economic progress and prosperity persisted. Working-class earnings climbed alongside those of the middle and upper classes. Automobile manufacturing was a key growth industry. The vehicle captivated Americans, profoundly altering their way of life. On the other hand, many reform efforts that had been so prevalent after 1900 began to fade in the 1920s.

The Progressive Era altered the United States in numerous ways that are still in use today. The American culture and people's welfare have improved due to many people's efforts, such as the Black Freedom

Movement, which Booker T. Washington and W.E.D. Influenced. Dubois. Many of the natural wonders that exist now were created by Roosevelt. After its initial failures, the Progressive Era assisted the United States in becoming a great country.

18/Roaring Twenties

The First World War, the Roaring twenties, and the Great Depression

In 1914, Germany, Austria-Hungary, and Turkey battled against the United Kingdom, France, Italy, and Russia. Other countries joined the battle, and the conflict spread over the Atlantic to affect the United States. The navies of the United Kingdom and Germany obstructed American shipments.

When a German submarine sunk the British ocean liner Lusitania in 1915, over 130 Americans were killed. President Woodrow Wilson urged that the German attacks stop.

They paused but resumed in 1917. The United States declared war on Iraq.

More than 1.7 million American soldiers aided in the defeat of Germany and Austria-Hungary. On November 11, 1918, a truce was reached in Versailles in France, formally ending the war.

President Wilson devised a 14-point peace plan, which included the formation of the League of Nations. He thought that the League would keep the peace, but the war's victors insisted on heavy retribution in the Treaty of Versailles. The United States did not even support the League of Nations.

Most Americans now embrace the United States' active involvement globally, but at the time, many did not.

Following the war, the United States faced racial tensions, failing farms, and labour unrest.

Next to Russia's Revolution in 1917, Americans were concerned about the development of communism. This is usually referred to as the Red Scare.

Nonetheless, the United States had an era of prosperity. Many families bought their first car, radio, or refrigerator. They watched a movie.

In 1920, women were granted the right to vote for the first time, and the good days ended in October 1929, when the stock market crashed and the economy entered a slump. The Great Depression was a worldwide economic depression that began in 1929 and lasted until about 1939. It was the longest and most severe slump that the industrialized Western world has ever seen, causing significant changes in economic institutions, macroeconomic policy, and economic theory. Despite its origins in the United States, the Great Depression brought sharp losses in output, widespread unemployment, and severe deflation in practically every country on the planet. Its social and cultural consequences were no less devastating, particularly in the United States, where the Great Depression was the toughest setback Americans had endured since the Civil War. That year, presidential contenders argued about how to end the Great Depression. The broad price deflation observed in the United States was also observed in other nations. Between 1929 and 1933, almost every industrialized country saw wholesale price decreases of 30% or more.

The United States began to improve in the spring of 1933. In the mid-1930s, output expanded rapidly: real G.D.P. increased at an annual pace of 9 per cent between 1933 and 1937. However, output had plummeted so precipitously in the early 1930s that it stayed far below its long-run trend line during this time. The United States saw another severe depression in 1937–38, but from mid-1938, the American economy expanded even faster than in the mid-1930s. In 1942, the country's output finally restored to its long-run trend line.

The harshness of the Great Depression in the United States is highlighted when contrasted to America's second-worst recession, the Great Recession of 2007–09. The country's real G.D.P. fell by just 4.3 per cent, and the unemployment rate peaked at less than 10%.

Herbert Hoover, the President at the time of the

crash, was defeated by Franklin D. Roosevelt.

*19/ The Causes of The Great Depression / F.D.R.
Memorial Site*

*20/ Florence Owens Thompson, aka Migrant Mother
by Dorothea Lange*

The New Deal and World War II

Because of unemployment and instability, President Roosevelt concluded that democracy had failed in other nations. He suggested a "New Deal" to end the Great Depression in the early 1930s.

Before Roosevelt's second term was underway, his domestic agenda was overshadowed by a new threat that most Americans were unaware of: the expansionist plans of totalitarian governments in Japan, Italy, and Germany. As Germany, Italy, and Japan maintained their aggressiveness, the U.S. declared that no country participating in the fight could rely on it for assistance. From 1935 to 1937, neutrality rules barred commerce with or credit to any of the belligerent states. The initial American response to the start of the war in Europe in 1939 was likewise neutrality.

Many programs were included in the New Deal. Bank accounts were protected. The stock market has been subjected to new regulations. To preserve their rights, workers might organize unions. Farmers received financial assistance for certain crops. The government recruited people to plant trees, clean up streams, and repair national parks. Skilled labourers assisted in the construction of dams and bridges. The government supplied flood control and electric electricity to low-income communities. The Social Security system assisted the impoverished and crippled, and many Americans were sceptical of large government, but they also wanted the government to assist regular citizens. These programs were beneficial, but they did not address the underlying economic issues. The next world war would accomplish that.

With the tumble of France and the air war against Britain in 1940, the discussion between those who supported supporting democracies and those who opposed it heated up. In the end, the interventionist argument was victorious. The United States joined Canada in establishing a Mutual Board of Defense and joined the Latin American republics in extending collective security to Western Hemisphere states. Congress appropriated massive funds for rearmament and, in early 1941, approved the Lend-Lease Program, which allowed President Roosevelt to send weaponry and equipment to any nation (particularly the United Kingdom, the Soviet Union, and China) deemed critical to the United States' defence.

While Germany, Italy, and Japan attacked other

countries, the United States stayed neutral. Even though many people hoped to avoid these battles, Congress opted to conscript soldiers and increase the military. Japan threatened to grab raw materials required by Western businesses as it gained areas in China and elsewhere in Asia. As a result, the U.S. refused to export oil to Japan. The United States supplied 80 per cent of Japan's oil. When the United States insisted that Japan withdraw from the lands it had acquired, Japan refused. Japan launched an attack on the American navy at Pearl Harbor, Hawaii, on December 7, 1941. Japan was declared a state of war by the United States. Because Germany and Italy were Japan's allies, they declared war on the United States.

American business was devoted to the war effort. While men became warriors, women manufactured 300,000 aeroplanes, 5,000 cargo ships, and 86,000 tanks.

The United States fought alongside Britain and the Soviet Union in Europe against the German Nazi menace.

Millions of people perished when Germany and the Soviet Union invaded Poland in 1939 (Germany attacked the Soviet Union in 1941) and the German capitulation in 1945. Millions more died due to the Holocaust, the Nazi regime's wholesale slaughter of Jews and other groups.

Even after the war in Europe finished, fighting persisted in Asia and the Pacific Ocean. These were among the deadliest engagements for American soldiers. Even when U.S. forces reached the Japanese home islands, Japan refused to surrender. Some Americans believed that invading Japan would result in more deaths in both the United States and Japan. When the atomic bomb was ready, President Harry S. Truman opted to use it on two Japanese cities, Hiroshima and Nagasaki, to end the war without an invasion. In August 1945, World War II came to an end.

The world would soon be terrified of nuclear weapons considerably more powerful than the bombs unleashed against Japan.

*21 /President Roosevelt signs the Declaration of War
against Japan, December 1941*

The Cold War, Korea, and Vietnam

Following WWII, the United States and Great Britain had long-standing differences with the Soviet Union about the future of Europe, the majority of which had been liberated from Nazi control via their joint efforts. Each desired to construct regimes that were favourable to its interests.

Russia had been invaded twice in the previous 40 years, and the United States had been drawn into European conflicts that were not of its creation both times.

Each claimed that its system was the most secure and that its beliefs provided liberty, equality, and prosperity. This period of conflict between the United States and Russia is commonly referred to as the Cold War.

Many empires crumbled, and civil conflicts erupted in the aftermath of World War II. The U.S. desired stability, democracy, and free commerce. Because the United States believed that postwar economic instability would strengthen the appeal of communism, it donated huge sums of money to European nations, including the Soviet Union, to repair war damage and rebuild their economies. The Soviet Union and the communist countries of Eastern Europe declined the offer. By 1952, the United States had committed $13.3 billion to reconstruct Western Europe through the Marshall Plan.

The Soviet military imposed communist administrations on Central and Eastern European states. The U.S. wished to restrain Soviet growth. It urged the departure of the Soviet Union from northern Iran.

America backed Turkey and assisted Greece in its struggle against communist insurgencies. When the Soviets blockaded West Berlin, a massive airlift from the United States delivered millions of supplies to the divided city.

Mao Zedong's communist armies gained control of China in 1949. In 1950, communist North Korea entered South Korea with the help of China and the Soviet Union to conquer.

The United States received backing for military involvement from the United Nations, previously the League of Nations, and a brutal conflict raged on until 1953. Despite the signing of an armistice, U.S. forces remain in South Korea to this day.

The Vietnam War (1954–75) was a lengthy battle in which the communist government of North Vietnam and its supporters in South Vietnam, known as the

Viet Cong, were set against the government of South Vietnam and its main supporter, the United States. The "American War" in Vietnam (or, in full, the "War against the Americans to Save the Nation") was also part of a broader regional battle (see Indochina conflicts) and a manifestation of the Cold War between the U.S. and the Soviet Union and their respective allies.

The aim of North Vietnam, which had defeated the French colonial government of Vietnam in 1954, was to unite the whole nation under a single communist rule modelled after that of the Soviet Union, and China was at the core of the battle. The South Vietnamese administration, on the other hand, strove to keep Vietnam closer to the West. Military advisers from the United States, present in modest numbers during the 1950s, were employed significantly beginning in 1961, and active combat forces were launched in 1965. By 1969, the United States had over 500,000 military forces stationed in Vietnam.

The final U.S. military unit left Vietnam on March 29, 1973. The communists and South Vietnamese were already engaged in what the media dubbed the "postwar war." With varying degrees of accuracy, both sides claimed that the other side was consistently breaching the conditions of the peace treaties. The United States maintained its large military aid program to Saigon, but the President's power to influence events in Vietnam was severely limited. As Nixon's reputation deteriorated due to the Watergate scandal, Congress prevented military action in Vietnam.

North Vietnam captured South Vietnam in 1975. thousands of people perished in the conflict, while many Vietnamese "boat people" left their new communist government. Americans were split over the war and hesitant to enter further foreign battles.

22/ Korean Conflict. Men of the 3rd Battalion,

23/ Troopers at firebase

Cultural Renovation

At home, some Americans' life began to improve. Families increased, and some relocated from cities to distant areas where they could afford larger homes. Not many Americans were as prosperous. African Americans began a campaign to achieve equal treatment worldwide.

By 1960, the government had grown increasingly dominant. Throughout the 1950s, the federal government's civilian workforce remained stable at 2.5 million, and In the 1960s, federal spending topped $150 billion. Most Americans embraced the government's growing involvement, even if they differed about how far it should go. John F. Kennedy was elected President in 1960. He was the youngest President ever to be elected at the age of 43. Kennedy sought to provide strong leadership to spread economic advantages to all residents. Still, a razor-thin margin of victory constrained his mandate, and his policies were frequently limited and controlled.

The Supreme Court declared in 1954 that segregated schools for black children were unequal to those for white students and that they must be integrated. President Lyndon B. Johnson backed Rev. Martin Luther King Jr.'s nonviolent campaign for African Americans' civil rights and voting rights. Some black leaders, such as Malcolm X, advocated for more violent methods of transformation. New legislation abolished segregation and gave African Americans the right to vote. Many black Americans strived to enter the more wealthy middle class. While racial discrimination remained, African Americans had a better opportunity to live freely and healthily.

In October 1962, Kennedy confronted the most severe crisis of the Cold War: the Cuban Missile Crisis. When the Soviet Union placed nuclear missiles in Cuba, Kennedy imposed a quarantine to prevent Soviet ships from transporting other missiles to the island. He publicly demanded that the Soviets withdraw the weapons. After many days of tenseness, the Soviets backed down. After the Soviet Union launched Sputnik in 1957, space became a new battle-field for competition. In April 1961, they completed a string of victories in space by launching the first man into orbit around the Earth. President John F. Kennedy answered by promising that Americans would walk on the moon before the decagon.

They concluded a string of victories in space by launching the first man into orbit above the Earth in

April 1961. President Kennedy reacted by promising that Americans would walk on the moon before the decade was through, and Neil Armstrong did it in July 1969.

Kennedy, who was slain in 1963, did not survive to see this accomplishment. Lyndon B. Johnson, his successor, adopted much new legislation from the Kennedy plan, establishing social change initiatives he referred to as the "Great Society." The battle for equality among black Americans peaked in the mid-1960s.

In the 60s and 70s, many American women were dissatisfied that they did not have the same possibilities as males. Betty Friedan and Gloria Steinem were pioneers of a drive to reform legislation to compete equally with men in business and education. When not enough states passed a proposed constitutional amendment offering equal rights for women, it failed, but many new laws did give equal rights.

During President Johnson's six-year tenure, the United States' engagement in Vietnam increased. Although politicians tended to see the conflict as an essential struggle to counter communism on all fronts, an increasing proportion of Americans considered Vietnam to have no important American interest. On college campuses, protests against America's role in the undeclared war erupted.

President Johnson, who was becoming more unpopular, opted not to seek a second full term. In 1968, Richard Nixon was elected President. Nixon signed a peace pact with North Vietnam, among other diplomatic achievements. He established relations with the People's Republic of China and successfully pursued a detente strategy with the Soviet Union. As it became evident that Congress was preparing to impeach him for White House complicity in the Watergate cover-up, he resigned in 1974.

Native Americans sought to ensure that the government kept its previous pledges. They reclaimed tribal lands and water rights and lobbied for housing and school help. Ben Nighthorse Campbell became the first Native American to be elected to the Senate in 1992.

Hispanic Americans from Mexico, Central America, Puerto Rico, and Cuba also participated in politics. They stood up against bigotry. They were elected to posts at the local, state, and national levels.

Students demonstrated against the Vietnam War, prompting President Lyndon B. Johnson to initiate peace talks. Long hair, rock 'n' roll music, and illicit drugs were apparent emblems of some young people's "counter-culture" attitudes at the period.

Pollution has become a source of concern for Americans. In 1970, the first Earth Day was declared. The Environmental Protection Agency (E.P.A.) was established. Pollution is being decreased as a result of new legislation.

America's civilization was evolving. The United States was gradually accepting its heterogeneous population.

24 / Neil Armstrong as he walked on the moon, July 20, 1969

The Culmination of the 20th Century

The United States has long been a nation where diverse ideas and points of view compete to influence legislation and social change. In the 1980s, the liberal activity of the 1960s–1970s gave way to conservatism.

Conservatives desired less government, a strong national defence, and tax reduction. Supporters of President Ronald Reagan (1981–1989) think his actions contributed to the Soviet Union's demise and the end of the Cold War. On the other hand, American politics may shift quickly: Americans voted for the more liberal Bill Clinton as President in 1992.

When the election was so close in 2000, politics were more cruel than normal. A Supreme Court decision on disputed ballots in Florida assured George W. Bush's victory over Al Gore.

The September 11 attacks, also known as the 9/11 attacks, were a chain of plane hijackings and suicide attacks carried out in 2001 against targets in the United States by 19 militants affiliated with the Islamic extremist group al-Qaeda and were the deadliest terrorist attacks on American soil in U.S. history. The attacks on New York City and Washington, DC, caused widespread death and devastation and sparked a massive counterterrorism campaign in the United States. In New York, 2,750 people were murdered, 184 in the Pentagon and 40 in Pennsylvania (where one of the hijacked flights crashed as passengers attempted to reclaim the jet); all 19 terrorists were killed.

Khalid Sheikh Mohammed (commonly referred to simply as "K.S.M." in the subsequent 9/11 Commission Report and the media) spent his boyhood in Kuwait. He was the chief operational planner of the September 11 attacks. Khalid Sheikh Mohammed started engaged in the Muslim Brotherhood at the age of 16 and subsequently advanced to the United States to attend college, graduating from North Carolina Agricultural and Technical State University in 1986. Following that, he proceeded to Pakistan and then Afghanistan to conduct jihad against the Soviet Union, which had invaded Afghanistan in 1979.

Hundreds of thousands of people observed the assaults first-hand (many bystanders photographed or videotaped the events), and millions more watched the catastrophe unfold live on television. The footage of the attacks was repeated in the media countless times in the days that followed September 11, as were scenes of crowds of people, bereaved, meeting at "Ground Zero"—as the location where the towers once stood came to be generally known—some with photos of missing loved ones, hoping for some indication of their fate.

President Bush said in September 2001 that he wanted Osama bin Laden captured—dead or alive—and a $25 million reward was subsequently posted for information leading to bin Laden's execution or arrest. Bin Laden avoided arrest many times, notably in December 2001, when U.S. soldiers traced him to the mountains of Tora Bora in eastern Afghanistan. Bin Laden's trail then went cold, and he was believed to be hiding somewhere in the Afghan-Pakistan tribal territories.

U.S. intelligence finally tracked him down in Pakistan, where he was staying in the garrison city of Abbottabad, and on May 2, 2011, on instructions from U.S. Pres. A small U.S. Navy SEAL, Barack Obama, stormed his compound and shot and killed al-Qaeda leader Osama bin Laden.

Nonetheless, anti-war activists and many Democrats seized the opportunity to argue that the war on terror had failed, that Osama bin Laden was not apprehended, and that the mission in Afghanistan remained incomplete.

Terrorists came to Iraq following the invasion, and

violence raged on into 2004. However, detractors disregarded the reality that a free and democratic Iraq and Afghanistan had become the Middle East's first true Arab democracies. Al Qaeda was now being drawn into conflict there rather than on American territory.

Even though research teams could not locate the chemical and biological weapons that had resulted in U.N. sanctions, many specialists and Iraqi informants claimed that Saddam had transferred weapons of mass destruction out of the country shortly before hostilities began. Despite this, many minor traces of biological and chemical weapons were recovered in various sites, generally in artillery shells, proving that they existed at one point.

But, whether the weapons were relocated or were a gigantic lie by Saddam for the warped joy of tricking the U.S., one thing is certain: after 2003, he would never threaten any of his neighbours, let alone America. Moreover, Iraq would no longer serve as a training ground for hijackers.

By late 2004, Iraq was still far from becoming a stable society; Bin Laden had not been apprehended or killed, and with each new arrest of a terror suspect came the realization of new risks. Many terrorism specialists, however, believed that even if the corner had not been turned, it was, at the very least, insight. Even still, it is doubtful that Americans will revert to a 9/10 attitude very soon.

25/ Plumes of smoke billow from the World Trade Center towers

War on Terrorism and the Afghan war

The term "war on terrorism" refers to the global counter terrorism operation initiated by the United States in response to the terror attack of September 11, 2001. The war on terrorism was comparable to the Cold War in terms of scope, expenditure, and impact on international relations; it was intended to represent a new phase in global political relations and has had significant consequences for security, human rights, international law, cooperation, and governance.

The fight against terrorism was a multifaceted effort with practically infinite possibilities. Its military dimension included massive battles in Afghanistan and Iraq, covert actions in Yemen and elsewhere, large-scale military aid programs for friendly regimes, and significant increases in the military budget. Its intelligence component included institutional reorganization and significant increases in funding for America's intelligence-gathering capabilities, a global program to appre-

hend terrorist suspects and intern them at Guan-
tánamo Bay, expanded cooperation with foreign
intelligence agencies, and tracking intercepting
terrorist financing.

The detention of hundreds of terrorist suspects
around the world, the stoppage of further large-
scale terrorist attacks on the American mainland,
the overthrow of the Taliban regime and subsequent
closure of terrorist-training camps in Afghanistan,
the capture or eradication of many of al-senior
Qaeda's members, and increased levels of international cooperation in global counterterrorism efforts
were among the successes of the first years of the
war on terrorism.

By the time U.S. President George W. Bush was re-
elected in 2004, the costs of the war on terrorism
were becoming clear. In Iraq, U.S. forces deposed
Saddam Hussein's government in 2003, and U.S. war
planners underestimated the difficulties of establishing a functioning government from scratch, failing
to consider how this effort could be problematical by
Iraq's sectarian tensions, which had been suppressed
by Saddam's repressive regime but were unleashed
by his removal.

By the last years of Bush's administration, public
opinion had shifted sharply against his management
of the Iraq War and further national security concerns. This dissatisfaction aided Barack Obama, an

outspoken opponent of Bush's foreign policies, in his election to the presidency in 2008. The phrase "war on terrorism," which was still intimately connected with Bush policies, swiftly vanished from official communications under the new government.

Obama indicated explicitly in a 2013 address that the United States will forego a limitless, ill-defined "global war on terrorism" in favour of more concentrated efforts against specific hostile organizations. Under Obama, the conflicts in Iraq and Afghanistan were gradually drawn down. However, U.S. forces remained in both countries after Obama's administration in 2016.

The first phase of the Afghan conflict, which consisted of overthrowing the Taliban (the ultraconservative political and religious organization that dominated Afghanistan and offered asylum to al-Qaeda, the culprits of the September 11 attacks), lasted just two months. The second phase, which persisted from 2002 to 2008, was distinguished by a U.S. policy of militarily rescinding the Taliban while reconstructing the key institutions of the Afghan state. The third phase, a return to old-fashioned counterinsurgency doctrine, began in 2008 and was hastened by U.S. President Barack Obama's decision in 2009 to temporarily raise U.S. troops' presence in Afghanistan. The greater force was employed to carry out a plan to safeguard the populace from

Taliban assaults and assist rebels in their efforts to reintegrate into Afghan society. A schedule accompanied the policy to withdraw foreign forces from Afghanistan; security duties would be progressively handed over to the Afghan military and police beginning in 2011. The new method mainly failed to meet its objectives. Insurgent attacks and civilian losses remained persistently high, while many Afghan militaries and police forces taking up security responsibilities seemed unprepared to repel the Taliban.

The 13-year Afghanistan War was the longest war ever waged by the United States when the U.S. and NATO combat operations formally concluded in December 2014.

The question of leaving foreign forces in the nation after NATO combat operations ended remained unresolved until the second part of 2014. Before leaving office, Karzai, nearing the end of his presidency, refused to sign the Bilateral Security Agreement, and a protracted recount delayed his successor's election. Ashraf Ghani was inaugurated as President in late September 2014 and quickly signed the Bilateral Security Agreement. On December 28, 2014, the United States and NATO formally completed their combat operation in Afghanistan. Still, a reduced presence of roughly 13,000 troops remained to support and train Afghan troops until a drawdown was finalized in 2020.

A full withdrawal of U.S. soldiers, begun in 2020 and expected to last until 2021, anticipated the end of U.S. commitment to Afghanistan. Still, the rise of the Taliban during the drawdown left the nation in a similar state as when U.S. forces entered 20 years earlier.

26/ Afghan War

Conclusion

Although the initial terror of 9/11 has subsided, the assault served as a powerful reminder that buildings, no matter how significant they may be, are nothing more than concrete and steel.

The precious human lives they held attested, via their demise, that what endures are ideas.

In their attempt to break the "materialism" of the United States, Osama bin Laden's terrorists just reminded the world of the intangible's superiority over the physical and of the spiritual's superiority over the temporal. Terrorists unified a nation deeply divided by an election and elevated a president under fire to a position of historical grandeur by refocusing Americans' attention on freedom—and its adversaries.

The fatal flaw of bin Laden, like Hitler, Stalin, and even the nearsighted Spaniards of five centuries ago, was that they focused on the physical manifestations of the West's wealth, failing to recognize that wealth is merely a byproduct of other, more important qualities: initiative, inventiveness, hope, optimism, and, most importantly, faith. Over three centuries ago, people who landed in Virginia and Massachusetts were generally destitute, sometimes alone, and certainly without high titles or regal honours.

After they ploughed the fields and established their businesses, it was not the farms alone that enabled Benjamin Franklin's Philadelphia to thrive, nor trade alone that gave John Adams' Boston vitality. Plantations alone did not give birth to George Washington and Thomas Jefferson, nor did a legal system give birth to Alexander Hamilton and Abraham Lincoln. American resolve and drive, vision, and dedication were not derived from acquiring material goods, though obtaining goods was required.

Rather, grandeur sprang from an overwhelming conviction that this was, after all, the "city on a hill," the "last, greatest hope for mankind." The United States was and endured to be a source of optimism and a beacon of liberty.

The United States has evolved enormously since its humble beginnings as 13 little-known colonies. Its 300 million inhabitants represent practically every national and ethnic group on the planet. Economic, technological, cultural, and societal advancements continue. Americans live in a world that is interdependent and interrelated.

The United States is firmly bound to the principles

of its founding fathers. Among these are faith in individual liberty and democratic democracy and the promise of economic opportunity and advancement for all.

The task of the United States is to ensure that its principles of liberty, democracy, and opportunity remain safe and viable in the twenty-first Century.

Bibliography

1. A Patriot's History of the United States, from Columbus's great discovery to the war on terror.Larry Schweikart and Michael Allen; Published by the Penguin Group

2. The U.S.A. History in brief by Bureau of international information programs U S. department of state;http://usinfo.state.gov/

3. Encyclopædia Britannica, Inc. https://www.britannica.com/topic/history-of-United-States

4. A Brief Overview of the American Civil War; A Defining Time in Our Nation's History By James McPherson https://www.battlefields.org/learn/articles/brief-overview-american-civil-war

5. History of the United States; U.S. Diplomatic Mission to Germany /Public Affairs/ Information Resource Centers;https://usa.usembassy.de/history-growth.htm

6. Library of Congress; Classroom Materials at the Library of Congress; U.S. History Primary Source Timeline; Progressive Era to New Era,

1900-1929

7. The British Library;https://www.bl.uk/onlineg
allery/onlineex/uscivilwar/origins/origins.htm
l

8. A short history of the department of state;
https://history.state.gov/departmenthistory/s
hort-history/superpower

9. The Pre-Civil War Era (1815–1850) https://w
ww.sparknotes.com/history/american/precivi
lwar/context/

10. Library Of Congress; Colonial America (1492–
1763) https://www.americaslibrary.gov/jb/colo
nial

11. National Geographic Kids/ https://kids.nationa
lgeographic.com/geography/countries/article/
united-states

Picture Index

Division, Library of Congress.

7. George Washington 1789-1797 https://usa.use mbassy.de/images/washington.gif

8. The Peace Hat and The Tomb of the Unknown Revolutionary War Soldier/Flicker

9. The Thirteen Colonies (shown in red) in 1775, with modern borders overlaid/ Adapted from the National Atlas of the United States /New England (New Hampshire; Massachusetts; Rhode Island; Connecticut); Middle (New York; New Jersey; Pennsylvania; Delaware); Southern (Maryland; Virginia; North Carolina; South Carolina; and Georgia)

10. Philadelphia - Old City: Independence Hall - The Signing of the Constitution/Flickr

11. Francis Scott Key reaches out towards the flag in "The Star-Spangled Banner" by Percy Moran/- Credit: Moran, Percy. "The Star-Spangled Banner." Copyright 1913. Prints and Photographs Division, Library of Congress.

12. A miner strikes gold in California/Credit: "John Stone with Gold Mining Pan" ca. 1939. California Gold: Northern California Folk Music from the Thirties. Collected by Sidney Robertson Cowell, Library of Congress.

13. National Atlas of the United States/ The Territorial acquisitions of the United States, such as the Thirteen Colonies, the Louisiana Purchase,

British and Spanish Cession, etc.

14. Lincoln's Emancipation Proclamation was issued on January 1, 1863/Credit: The Strobridge
Lith. Co., Cincinnati." Abraham Lincoln and
his Emancipation Proclamation." c1888. Prints
and Photographs Division, Library of Congress.

15. Alexander Gardner's famous photo of Confed-
erate dead before the Dunker Church on the
Antietam Battlefield in Sharpsburg, Md., 1862.
Library of Congress

16. A depiction of San Juan Hill's storming from
the Spanish-American War/Credit: "William
H. West's Great Achievement, The Storming
of San Juan Hill." copyright 1899. Prints and
Photographs Division, Library of Congress.

17. George M. Cohan's song "Over There" captured
the patriotic mood of the time/Credit: Cohan,
George M. "Over There." Sheet Music. 1917.
Historic American Sheet Music, 1850-1920
(from Duke University), Library of Congress.

18. Roaring Twenties | (Photo: Gabriele Kantel) |
Jörg Kantel | Flickr

19. The Causes of The Great Depression / F.D.R.
Memorial Site | Flickr

20. Florence Owens Thompson, aka Migrant
Mother by Dorothea Lange

21. President Roosevelt signs the Declaration of
War against Japan, December 1941/Credit: Of-

fice of War Information. "President Roosevelt Signing the Declaration of War Against Japan." December 1941. By Popular Demand: Portraits of the Presidents and First Ladies, 1789-Present, Library of Congress.

22. Korean Conflict. Men of the 3rd Battalion, 34th Infantry Regiment, 35th Infantry Division, covering up behind rocks to shield themselves from exploding mortar shells, near the Hantan River in central Korea/ Photo by the Signal Corps, U.S. Army.

23. Troopers at firebase Gonder burning their bunker, Chinook carrying truck back to Vietnam, Sky troopers moving out from the jungle terminate their operation in Cambodia. —- Image by © Bettmann/CORBIS/flicker

24. "That's one small step for man... and one giant leap for mankind," said Neil Armstrong as he walked on the moon, July 20, 1969/Credit: Armstrong, Neil. "Astronaut Edwin E. Aldrin, Jr., Lunar Module Pilot of the First Lunar Landing Mission, Poses for a Photograph beside the Deployed United States Flag during an Apollo 11 Extravehicular Activity (E.V.A.) on the Lunar Surface." July 20, 1969, courtesy of the National Aeronautics and Space Administration.

25. Plumes of smoke billow from the World Trade Center towers in Lower Manhattan, New York

City, after a Boeing 767 hits each tower during the September 11 attacks. /https://commons.wikimedia.org/wiki/File:WTC_smoking_on_9-11.jpeg /Michael Foran

26. Afgan   Conflict/internationalaffairs.org.au. /C.P.L. Sam Shepherd

About the Author

Jagath Jayaprakash is an Author, Op-Ed Columnist and the Manager of the Multi-Disciplinary Research Center of the Indian Institute of Technology, Jammu. Numerous of his works have been released in both Malayalam and English. Several articles on Political history, National security, Cyberwarfare, and International relations have been published in popular news magazines and various news websites.